Seduction Spells

Teresa Moorey

Seduction Spells

with photography by Daniel Farmer

RYLAND
PETERS
& SMALL
LONDON NEW YORK

Senior Designer Sally Powell

Senior Editor Clare Double

Location Research Emily Westlake

Production Deborah Wehner

Art Director Gabriella Le Grazie

Publishing Director Alison Starling

Stylist Anna Unwin

Editorial Consultant Christina Rodenbeck

First published in the
United States in 2004
by Ryland Peters & Small, Inc.
519 Broadway
5th Floor
New York NY 10012
www.rylandpeters.com

10 9 8 7 6 5 4 3 2 1

ISBN 1 84172 618 4

Printed and bound in China

contents

Loving Number One   6

Mate Magnet   18

Tonight's the Night   34

Bed of Roses   50

picture credits   64

Loving

Number

One

To be attractive you have to feel attractive—so start with yourself. The spells in this chapter are designed to work on you alone. Magic starts in your mind. What you imagine takes shape on the astral plane and translates to everyday. To be sexy, you must FEEL sexy. There's no kidding Spirit!

On a "bad hair day," don't try to "think positive"—you can't force this. Instead, bypass your own negative thoughts and plug into the source of all magic, Nature herself. Connect your body to the bounty around you. Go for walks. Feel the sun on your skin. Taste a raindrop, breathe in flowers' scent. Go out into woodland and simply listen.

Your body is your precious possession, connecting you to the sensuous web surrounding you. The details don't matter. Fall in love with life and you will love yourself. And you will be ready to enchant!

Unknowingly, we often create barriers to love. Lower them with this spell.

Space to Seduce

You will need:
a white candle

pencil and paper

a deep pink candle

an ashtray

Light your white candle and sit before it, reflecting. What is keeping you from fulfillment? This could be fear, laziness, or many things. Be honest.

Write down everything you've thought about and twist the paper into a taper, visualizing all the negative things twisted up inside it.

Light the taper in the candle flame. Use it to light the pink candle, saying:

Stale and tiresome, now depart,
Open passage to my heart.
Warmth and pleasure now will be
In the dancing flame I see.

Burn the taper in the ashtray. Extinguish the white candle and gaze at the flame of the pink one, feeling its heat transferring to your own body, which is now glowing.

Throw the ashes outside. Repeat this spell when necessary.

Your body is a vehicle of pleasure.
Have a love-fest with Number One!

Beautiful Me

You will need:
lavender oil diluted two drops
per teaspoon in carrier oil

ingredients for a relaxing
evening (see spell)

First have a pampering soak. Next, spread a large
towel on your bed, and begin a self-massage. Gently
work the oil into your feet. Think of the wonderful
things they do, such as walk and dance. Say, "Feet, I
love you!" Work up your legs in the same way, saying,
"Legs, I love you," "Knees, I love you," and so on.
Continue up your body, reminding yourself of good
times. If unpleasant thoughts occur, stop, smile, and
let them pass before continuing. Linger on any part
of you that needs extra attention.

Afterwards, relax as you please. Have fruit, chocolate,
a glass of wine, listen to music, or watch the stars.

Repeat once a month to retain that special feeling.

We all radiate a corona of energy or "aura." This spell will charge up your aura so you feel great!

Aura of Desire

You will need:

a piece of carnelian, cleansed in salt water

red wine or red juice

six red candles

a cinnamon incense stick

Place the carnelian in your drink. Bathe or shower, and remain naked. Light the candles and incense stick and place them around you.

Stand and extend your arms. Visualize your aura around you—it's most intense close to your body. Concentrate on it and imagine it glowing stronger.

Drink the liquid, being careful not to swallow the stone. Imagine the fiery elixir flowing through your body. Convey this to your aura. You are a radiant being, a vessel for joy!

Let the incense burn out. Cleanse the carnelian in a stream or bottled spring water and leave it in sunlight for a few hours, to prepare it for reuse. Go out and shine!

Secure your powers, and strut your stuff with style!

Knot of Love

You will need:
three cords representing
three things you like about
yourself. Choose suitable
colors, for example, red, if
you prize your energy

patchouli oil

Cut the cords to fit your waist. Anoint each with a drop of oil. Hold them with their ends together and make knots along the "rope" as you chant:

Knot of one, my spell's begun
Knot of two, something new
Knot of three, this spell shall be
Knot of four, more and more
Knot of five, the spell's alive!
Knot of six, this spell I fix
Knot of seven, earth and heaven
Knot of eight, the hand of fate
Knot of nine, the spell is mine!

Your first and last knots should come close to the ends of the cords. Wear your knotted cords as a girdle or place them in your wardrobe. You've got it all tied up!

Mate

Magnet

Hopefully, you now love yourself. You are glowing with self-esteem and vibrating with sensuous awareness! The time has come to turn your magical efforts to attracting a mate.

You want to get into a relationship—and get horizontal! However, it is important not to direct your magic at a particular person, however desirable they may seem, for it is against the ethics of witches to influence the life-path of another. It also tends to have a nasty way of rebounding! So visualize the kind of love, passion, sex, and person to have it with, but try not to be specific.

Be open-minded. We all change and we are all full of surprises. If you are determined you want someone tall and dark, you might miss the signals from someone fair—and sizzling between the sheets! Concentrate on how you want to feel—and brew up a storm!

Bag the grooviest gear for your mate-hunt.

Getting the Gear

You will need:

lavender soap or bath oil

lavender body lotion

two magnets

pictures of cool clothes

dill or fennel seeds

Shopping is fun! Mercury is the god of commerce, so get him on your side. First, bathe using lavender oil or soap, for lavender is ruled by Mercury. Visualize yourself returning with just the right thing. Dry yourself and massage the lotion all over you. Don't get dressed.

Take one of the magnets and pass it over your body. You are a magnet for sexy clothes! Pass the other magnet over the pictures of the gear you want. Don't be so specific that you limit the magic.

Join the magnets, opposite poles together. Mission accomplished!

Place your magnets on your lust shrine (see page 27), if you like. As you go off to the stores, scatter the seeds to the wind as an offering to Mercury.

A good talisman draws what you desire
—in this case a good roll in the hay!

Turn-you-on Talisman

You will need:
some red cloth in nonfray fabric

a laundry marker pen

dried dill

needle and thread

Cut two circles of cloth, the right size to fit in a bag or pocket. Think of three sexy things about your body or personality. Imagine them symbolically—sexy legs could be the number 11, cheerfulness a smiley face.

Draw your designs on one of the cloth circles, and the signs for Venus and Mars (the male and female signs) on the other. If you're gay, do one of the symbols twice. Hold the cloths between your palms and pour into them your lustful imaginings.

If you wish, stroke a little love-juice onto the inside of the cloth with your finger. Place the dill between the cloths and sew them together. Carry your talisman with you, to maximize your pulling power.

Make a shrine to lust—somewhere to work your seduction spells and keep useful magical items.

Lust Shrine

You will need:

a cupboard top or shelf in a suitable place

a deep red cloth to cover it

sexy items of your choice!

Choose red candles to call the Lust Deities. Find a sexy picture and representations of sex, such as a twig passed through a ring, lozenge-shaped artefacts for the vagina, phallic ones for the penis—anything that takes your fancy but is also tasteful and attractive to look at. Acorns, vanilla beans, mint, and rosemary are all linked to lust. Add a statue of Eros, the Horned God of Wiccans, or Venus/Aphrodite.

Tend your altar with flowers and incense, if possible containing cinnamon, vanilla, rosemary, galangal, or patchouli. If you are going out on the prowl, you might like to leave your underwear in front of your goddess or god figures beforehand, as a dedication.

All acts of love and pleasure are rituals of the Goddess!

Make your handshake armed and dangerous—to celibacy!

Horny Handshake

You will need:
non-magical basics—
clean nails and skin

a ring (optional,
see spell)

Standing before your shrine, practice visualizing. Select a simple, erotic image. Build your arousal and send the sexy electricity down your arm.

When a desirable person offers his or her hand, look them in the eye. Hold the hand firmly and gently, for just a nano-second longer than necessary. Imagine your erotic image sending the charge down your arm, as you have practiced.

If you wish, choose a serpent ring or one set with carnelian, garnet, bloodstone, or ruby. Consecrate the ring by passing it through the smoke of one of the incenses mentioned on page 27, and leave it before your deity while a red candle burns, for about an hour. Passion is within your grasp!

You will need:

a stone

a lavender incense stick

a red candle

a blue bowl containing water

a wand made from a rosebush twig

It's Elementary

Get the elements on your side!

Place the stone in the North, the burning incense stick in the East, the lit candle in the South, and the water in the West. Starting in the North and turning clockwise, form a circle around you with your wand.

Again facing North, hold your wand over the stone, saying, "Powers of Earth, give me gifts of the Body." Hold your wand over the incense stick and say, "Powers of Air, bring me gifts of the Mind!" Hold the wand over the candle. Say, "Powers of Fire, give me gifts of the Imagination." Hold your wand over the water and say, "Powers of Water, give me gifts of the Emotions."

Face North again. Thank each quarter. The Source be with you!

Draw your lover to you
with this sensual shimmy.

Dance of Desire

You will need:
perfume

seven gauzy veils

four red candles

incense (see page 27)

one long cord

a symbol of the kind of lover
you want, perhaps a sketch

something to attach the symbol
to the cord

sexy music

Bathe, apply perfume, and wind the veils around you. Light the candles in the corners of the room and burn the incense. Stretch out the cord and attach the lover-symbol SECURELY to the far end.

Play the music and dance sensuously. One by one, unwind the veils until you are naked. Imagine the desirable person looking at you.

Still dancing, pull on the cord. Imagine your lover being pulled towards you, irresistibly. Wrap the cord round your waist. Hold the symbol by your genitals as you finish the dance.

Sleep with the cord round your waist and the symbol between your thighs. Sweet dreams!

Tonight's the Night

Once that hot date's in the bag, consenting adults can take magical help. What you really want is most important. If you have doubts, repeat the "Beautiful Me" spell on page 12 and let the evening take care of itself.

How well do you know yourself? Has the thought of a night of passion blinded you to the emotional fallout? Cunning witches care for themselves!

Light a white candle and jasmine incense on your Lust Shrine, and ask Aphrodite to guide you. Imagine an arch of red roses. Beyond it, a mist clears to reveal a path, symbol, or person. If there is a path, follow it until you see something important (its meaning may not be instantly obvious).

Come back to everyday awareness and take time to feel clear. You know what to do—nothing can stop you now!

This shower spell will raise the sizzle factor.

Sexy Shower

You will need:
two teaspoons of dried lavender

a vanilla bean

three cinnamon sticks

a square of white cloth

some red ribbon

a red candle

Place the herbs on the cloth, while you chant:

Lavender so fresh and clean
Wash off all that comes between.
Vanilla so warm and sweet
Bring your gift of passion's heat.
Sacred wood of cinnamon
Fire this night—my will be done.

Place your palms over the herbs, sending lustful imaginings into them. Chant again as you tie the corners of the cloth up with some of the ribbon, and again as you hang the bag from the showerhead.

As you shower, imagine each droplet making you sparkle with sensuality. It doesn't matter if only a little water comes through the bag.

Light the candle as you get ready. You're almost too hot to handle!

Apples are associated with love rites—and we all know Eve tempted Adam with an apple!

Saucy Apples

You will need:

a knife

two rosy apples

a skewer

lemon juice

some red ribbon

cider

This spell is best used on someone who consents. Carve your name into the skin of one apple and your lover's into the other. Make a "tunnel" through both apples with the skewer. Sprinkle lemon juice on the carving and tunnel openings to stop them going brown.

Thread the ribbon through the tunnels. Tie the apples cheek to cheek. Place them on your shrine before your deity, and drink a cider toast to physical bliss.

Share the apples with your lover if you can, or eat them yourself. Untie the ribbon and use it to tie one of each of your wrists loosely together. Cut each apple in half horizontally, revealing the magical five-point "star" at the center. Feed the halves to each other with your free hands, making sure you both eat half of the same apple. Mmm!

Shape figures of yourself and the object of your desires. It's up to you how explicit you want to be!

Figure it Out

You are going to shape your dream lover. How precise do you want to be? Are you sure a certain someone can't get you off their mind? Or should you be non-specific? Don't kid yourself—all you do comes back to you!

Use self-hardening clay or modeling clay.

First make an effigy of yourself, inserting hair or nail clippings (keep it safe—it is a strong representation of you). Decorate it, using your imagination. You might scratch your name or just paint the head with your hair color.

The other figure could be a phallic or yonic shape, with inscriptions describing your ideal lover, or it might be a non-specific human shape. Or you may want to identify it in similar ways to your own. Whichever, set it with yours in a love-making posture.

Place the figures on your Lust Shrine and anoint them with lavender and patchouli oil. Say, "I anoint these in honour of ... (god/dess). Of earth they are made, earth make real my desires." Leave them in place and light a red candle each night—until you are satisfied!

Be deliciously aware of the power of your own sexuality.

Strip Tease

You will need:

one thick candle

seven deep pink candles

a large glass of red wine or red juice

a wand made from a rose stem or apple wood

seven veils or scarves

rose oil

sexy music

Light the thick candle. Place your pink candles, the glass of wine, and wand nearby. Anoint each veil with rose oil, draping them around you.

Dance to the music, imagining your lover watching. Unwind the first veil, encircling one of the candles with it. Light that candle from the large one. Do the same with each veil and candle, imagining your lover's arousal mounting.

When you are naked, sit by candlelight with the wineglass between your thighs. Thrust the wand into the wine, saying, "The masculine wand plunges into the feminine chalice." (Adapt this for gay sex.)

Lick the wand clean and drink the wine. Repeat this in front of the real person—if you dare!

*Create a fragrance that is
a magical essence of you.*

Scent of the Chase

You will need:
two red candles

patchouli oil

a red glass bowl

spring water

a teaspoon of caraway seeds

a pinch of saffron

nine rose petals

your favorite perfume

Perform this spell over seven days of the waxing moon, culminating at full moon. Anoint the candles with patchouli oil. Fill the bowl with spring water. Add the herbs, rose petals, nine drops of your scent, some of your saliva, and some love-juice.

Place the candles so their flames are reflected in the water. Burn them each evening, bringing them closer each time until they are side by side. Tilt them together, merging the flames. Hold them steady, watching the united reflection. Say, "'I have my desire."

Strain and bottle the water. Bury what's left of the candles, along with the herbs and petals. Apply the water with your usual scent on that special date.

Stir up this hot potion before a date.

Hot Chocolate

You will need:
milk

a vanilla bean

hot chocolate or cocoa powder

brown sugar

your rose or apple wand
(see page 44)

a cocktail stick

marshmallows

Simmer the milk gently with the vanilla bean in a pan. Make up the hot chocolate following the instructions on the package, and add sugar to taste.

Stir the chocolate with the tip of your wand. Trace images on the frothy surface—anything lusty and sensuous—while imagining seducing your lover. Say,

I stir this potion of love so sweet
And so my desire becomes complete.

Pour the chocolate into a mug. Using the cocktail stick, scratch symbols or letters on the marshmallows to signify something you want from your love-making, for instance L for lick.

Drop the marshmallows into your mug, saying the message on each three times. Watch them melt into the rich, creamy drink, and sip slowly. Yummy!

Bed of
Roses

That longed-for night is approaching and you want to make it really fabulous. Once you know your feelings are returned, you can do your wicked best to arouse. You might like to include your lover in some of the spells. Making a love-demon together, for instance, could form part of your sex games.

It is important to take action in the non-magical world, too. Consolidate your spells with all the usual things—dressing to kill, an intimate dinner for two, soft music.

When we perform magic we are using our own drives as a power source. There are few stronger feelings than that of sexual desire. A good spell will also have a strong effect on the spellcaster, and in the case of lust-magic, this is hardly surprising, bearing in mind the visualizations involved! Why hold back? Fill your kinky boots!

Spread this sensual sheet on your bed to entice that fabulous partner!

Lust Sheet

You will need:

a red, deep pink, or black sheet, preferably new and made from natural fibers

a large bowl, preferably red

enough spring water to immerse your sheet

essential oils of patchouli, cinnamon, and rose or vanilla

Wash the sheet, then rinse it in a clear, running stream or bottled spring water.

Fill the bowl with spring water. Dissolve three drops of oil of patchouli, six drops of cinnamon, and seven of rose or vanilla. Stir clockwise, saying,

Turn, turn, turn, and turn
Water cool, and passion burn,
Turn, turn, turn, and turn.

Gaze into the water and imagine passionate scenes. Chant again.

Immerse the sheet in the enchanted water for 24 hours. Let it dry naturally—if possible in the light of the full moon. Spread it lovingly on your bed.

Native American dream-catchers draw good dreams to the sleeper. Try this sexy variation.

Dreamboat-Catcher

You will need:
deep red ribbon

a wooden embroidery hoop, approx. 5 inches in diameter

thick red thread

glue or a large-eyed needle

two feathers

some of your pubic hair—and some of your lover's, if possible!

sexy symbols (see spell)

Thinking about sex, wind the ribbon around the hoop and secure by gluing or sewing. Next, weave a web within the hoop. Take the thread from one side to the other by sewing the thread to the binding, or tying it. Fix a ribbon for hanging and dangle the feathers on ribbons from the bottom. Weave in the hairs and thread or glue your symbols to the web. They could be hearts, acorns, sexy shapes, dried roses or violets, cinnamon sticks, rosemary sprigs, jewels, pictures, or anything you like. Your dream-catcher doesn't have to look good to be effective!

Hang the dream-catcher over the bed and let it capture you a night of erotic dreams come true!

A "poppet" is a magical image, made of wax or a similar material. Ours is naughty, but nice!

Love Poppet

You will need:

wax, self-hardening clay, modeling clay, or ginger root to shape into the figure

hair and/or nail clippings of consenting person/s concerned

a white candle

patchouli oil

Make the poppet in your lover's image to fire their desires for you, if you wish, or you can make a poppet love-demon, to send you both crazy!

Add the hair or clippings to the poppet—if you are using ginger, cut slits for them. "Dress" or adorn the figure in suitable ways—use your imagination!

Light a white candle on your shrine, hold the poppet, and say, "I name you … ." "Baptise" it with patchouli oil.

Caress your poppet. If it's your lover, tell him or her what you are going to do to them, if it is a demon, tell it what it will bring to your love-making. Take your poppet to bed—oooh!

If you don't have an (X-rated) dream then you can't have a dream come true!

Erotic Dreams

You will need:
small squares of pink tissue paper

a red pen

lavender or rose oil

Think of all the things you would like your lover to do to you, or you to him or her. Think also of how you would like to feel, and what you would like as an outcome. Write each wish onto a piece of tissue with the red pen, anoint each corner of the paper with a little oil, and crumple it up. You can make as many of these little "packages" as will fit under your pillow. Just make sure none of your wishes are mutually exclusive!

Place the packages under your pillow inside your pillowcase, while you sleep alone, or use them to charge things up with that sexy someone. You won't sleep a wink!

It doesn't take much imagination to link a candle with all sorts of lusty thoughts!

Sexy Candle

You will need:

two pink candles

a candle holder

a thick red or deep pink candle

rose petals

essential oils of rose, plus lavender (for a male lover) or patchouli (for a female lover)

a small red stone

red cloth

Light two pink candles on your shrine (see page 27), to work by. Play sensuous music. By your lust deity, place a holder for the thick candle, with the rose petals around it. Undress and rub the candle over your body.

Rub a few drops of the oils into the candle. Embed the red stone in the candle, close to the wick. Light the candle. As the wax melts, chant

Lust be mine, passion mine,
Fire and tenderness, night divine
Bodies in true bliss entwine
Lust be mine, passion mine.

Continue chanting until the stone drops into the petals. Wrap the stone and petals in the red cloth and place under your pillow.

PICTURE CREDITS

All photography by Daniel Farmer except:

Pages 8–9 photographer Melanie Eclare/
"La Bergerie," the Luxembourg garden of
Marc Schoellen (garden historian and amateur
garden designer), t. +352 327 269

Page 49 photographer Martin Brigdale